Reflections of the Early Hollywood Years

Anthony Taylor

A publication of

Eber & Wein Publishing

Pennsylvania

Reflections of the Early Hollywood Years

Copyright © 2017 by Anthony Taylor

Library of Congress
Cataloging in Publication Data

ISBN 978-1-60880-592-1

Proudly manufactured in the United States of America by

Eber & Wein Publishing

Pennsylvania

Reflections of the Early Hollywood Years

Reflections of the Early Hollywood Years

In March of 1997, I decided to try something different and unique. I decided to give show business a chance as a career, because my regular evening job was not promising a move up with a college degree.

At the present time, I do not recall how I found this agency. I think I might have located the agency through a local Manhattan newspaper that was popular at that time.

The photographer was very supportive of my new career, and my looks. He informed me his agency would contact me if a job offer should come in for me.

A couple weeks later, a call came for me to appear in a major motion picture called *Godzilla*. I was informed my part would be as an extra in the movie. I was told that the shoot would take place outside in the Wall Street area of New York City.

On the actual day of the shoot, I was excited; I was overjoyed and felt like Heaven had opened its doors to me and said *come in, my child!*

As I walked to the set, thousands of thoughts passed through my mind. I wondered if I would be the next male Lucille Ball—or the next Clarke Cable with my very distinguish mustache. I wondered if I would be the next rising star in Hollywood. Would they welcome me and my talent? On that day, I wondered and I wondered.

On the actual set of *Godzilla*, they provided rain through the rain machines. I will never forget that shoot, because we were drenched in rain, despite the fact we had raincoats.

In January 1998, I am pleased to say I worked in another major motion picture entitled *The Astronaut's Wife*. I worked as an extra, and the filming took place in the New York Public Library System on 42nd St. and Fifth Ave.

I enjoyed that shoot very much because it was inside. The shoot was not as long as the one for *Godzilla*. Both jobs paid well at the time; however, neither scene in which I appeared was used in the films.

Being an extra allows you to comprehend the film and acting industry from the bottom. You see different people from all walks of life, all with different acting experiences and capabilities.

I met professionals from various careers. Unfortunately, I have not had the pleasure to work with them again.

My next big job came to me in acting, not as an extra, but as an actor having a major role in a television commercial. The Television Network was MTV.

The shoot lasted two days: June 30,1999, and July 1, 1999. I played a doctor buying groceries in a supermarket.

On the same shoot, the next scene was in a restaurant, and the last scene was in the park.

In the park, I was swinging in a seat with a big, big smile. I was told by the director that I would receive a copy of the VHS cassette in the mail; however, I never did receive it! That was the biggest Hollywood production at that time, and it paid a great deal of money.

I never saw that commercial on MTV, because I did not get cable until the twenty-first century.

During July of 1999, I participated in my third major motion picture as an extra. The picture was titled *For Love of the Game*. It starred Kevin Costner as a baseball player.

The shoot took place at Yankee Stadium in the city of the Bronx in New York State.

That was my longest shoot to date: fourteen hours, minus one hour for lunch.

My career as a songwriter and poet also took off during these years. In 1999, I had a total of six albums to my credit— six songs written by Anthony Taylor on each individual album.

I am currently the Chairman of the Board at HSATP Corp located in Brooklyn, NY. The Corp, under my direction, has two chapbooks that are currently published, ready for purchase. There are two songs on iTunes that were originally published under Holland Song Publishing Company; that company has been converted into a corporation. The two songs are "I Got Her Back in My Arms Again" and "How Do You Do It, When You Do It, Every Time You Do It, When It Is So Satisfying to Me."

These songs, hopefully, will bring royalties to the corp.

My early career in Hollywood was a tremendous success up until the terrorist attacks on the World Trade Center (and certain parts of the United States).

Despite the fact I was gaining in years, there was work for me to do pertaining to the performing arts. I worked my full-time job and my Hollywood career on the side—acting, modeling, and writing songs.

On September 11, 2001, New York City, the rest of the United States, and the whole wide world were put on edge when terrorists hijacked two planes and crashed each one into the towers of the World Trade Center.

Shocked, horrified, stunned, and in disbelief, the United States and the world was put into a tailspin. Who would ever think that someone would deliberately attack the United States on its own civilian soil?

My co-workers at the job were in disbelief. As I informed you earlier, when I worked on *Godzilla* back in 1997, I felt like I was in Heaven to be working on the movie lot filming; however, September 11, 2001 changed all that. Opportunities to work in the film industry were minimal. People were more concerned about the aftermath of the terrorists' attacks on the World Trade Center, the Pentagon in Washington, D.C., and the airplane crashing into the countryside presumed to be heading towards the White House or Capitol Building of the United States.

This written historical piece is not about September 11, 2001, but about my early years in Hollywood before the horrific attacks on the World Trade Center and the United States.

Unfortunately, these terrorist attacks affected my career in an unfavorable manner—pertaining to my early Hollywood years.

It was during this time period that I was asked to become a member of the Board of Trustees at Cornerstone Baptist Church in Brooklyn, New York. The years in office were January 2001 through January 2007.

My years as a trustee at Cornerstone were inspirational, spiritual, and educational. Pastor Wright asked me to be a trustee at his Church in December 2000.

I thought about his offer and wondered if I could keep a commitment for six years serving with Christian discipline and respect within a religious office position.

I decided to take his offer, because I never really did serve a position within the church, and I did it as to acknowledge the hardship and suffering of the Black race upon these shores. If it were not for certain Black political and spiritual leaders, most of my accomplishments could not have been done.

The Black church has always been the background or foundation for the spiritual renewal of the Black American on these shores of America.

Despite slavery, reconstruction, Jim Crow, the Harlem Renaissance, and the Civil Rights Movement of the 1960s, the church has always stood as one foundation for the Black race.

My parents introduced me to the Black church. As a child, I used to go to Mass at a Catholic church with my sister. She grew up during the era of the Civil Rights Movement of the 1960s. She was very popular as a teenager, especially the teenagers who attended the Catholic church.

I remember a little of the Mass services from the mid- to late-1960s. The services were held early in the morning.

Well, that's enough facts from that era. I could write a book on that era alone.

Being on the Board of Trustees at my church was inspirational and educational. I learned how to count and manage *holy* money without the temptation of stealing. I knew it was the Lord's money that parishioners and members contributed to the functioning of the church.

As I was a member, I saw trustees come and go! When it was my turn to come off the board, my feelings were hurt when my mother did not come to see me to receive my plaque for the time and services I gave to the board for six years.

She stated the trip from the South to the North would be too much for her during her age in history. I accepted her explanation; that is also another story!

With the terror attacks on the United States, and the completion of my time on the Board of Trustees at Cornerstone Baptist Church, my work experience began to pick up a little in Hollywood, California. My book, *Human Expressions* was published in 2002, one year after I was on the board.

I published two books. *Human Expressions* sold the most copies of the two to date. There were numerous book signings at Cornerstone Baptist Church and at my place of work at the VA Hospital.

In 2008, I was approached to participate in the audience on *The People's Court*. A talent agency landed me the job. I received pay for the days I was on camera and in the audience. The shoot was recorded mostly in the mornings and then some in the afternoons.

This was the only Hollywood production that gave me the dates and times of the recordings for *The People's Court*—from the live studio audience to television—to allow the actors/extras to make hard copies of the recorded broadcast(s).

Thank God, as an actor and extra, I was able to record the shows from *The People's Court* to a hard copy on VHS format. Even more amazing, on many of the shows, you can see me, Anthony Taylor, in the background the *The People's Court*.

To this day, I remember a veteran from my day job informing me that he saw me on *The People's Court*. The veteran described the exact wardrobe I was wearing, even the color. I was impressed with his exact description.

That experience on *The People's Court* enlightened my Hollywood experience, because I had a copy of my own work to show people at that time in history.

Well, the year is now 2009, and 2008 has passed. After many accomplishments, offers for jobs in Hollywood were minimal after the terrorist attacks on the United States.

I do remember the next-to-last job I had in Hollywood before I reached middle-age. The particular job was for a commercial for PK Network.

The PK Network was a cable station that geared its entertainment to family and its values. I remember this particular job because it paid a nice sum of money at that time in history.

I posed as a husband with a wife and one child. The production of this project took place in June 2009. After the death of my mother in 2010, and with my old age, my career in Hollywood spiraled downward to another level.

I still continued to write poems and songs. Eventually, I started to write villanelles and short stories. I truly, truly missed those days when I was placed in front of those huge, gigantic cameras that captured me on screen; I felt as if I were a star in the Milky Way Galaxy, or someone of high importance.

Leaving from the early years in Hollywood to another era, I published another book myself, and the publisher was Dorrance. It was entitled *Let's Go on a Sentimental Journey.*

This was another book pertaining to a collection of poems dedicated to past events and persons. *Let's Go on a Sentimental Journey* is the last big Hollywood production to date; the book was released in the year 2011.

In 2011, I joyfully entered a master's degree program at the now-closed Jones International University. I focused on business communications—such as writing, speech, and digital video recordings. I completed the program in the year 2014. The Graduation Exercises were held in 2015.

As I come to the conclusion of this writing pertaining to the early Hollywood years of Anthony Taylor, I continue to write poetry in chapbook form(s), and have my own poetry show on YouTube. The poetry show is produce by my own company—CJFC Studios.

At the present, this is the only major production of CJFC Studios. Eventually, in the future, it is hoped that more productions will be produced at CJFC Studios.

For me, at the present time, there are no more notes to write pertaining to my early Hollywood years in the performing arts. The sun has begun to set on that part of my empire.

However, a role might be offered here and there in the distant future. Who is to say? I might be another William Shakespeare or Langston Hughes.

Photographs of Anthony Taylor

The Early Hollywood Years

Looking like a star with my Madonna T-shirt from the 1980s. This picture was taken at my first photo shoot (1997).

ANTHONY TAYLOR

My very first headshot—I was so proud of this achievement. It was a new step into a new direction.

Another headshot photographed during my third photo shoot in the early 2000s.

A nice black-and-white picture of me as a model.

Another picture taken as I leave my early Hollywood years behind.

Another headshot of me as I head into the sunset of my Hollywood career.

Trustee Anthony Taylor
Cornerstone Baptist Church
2001–2007

A professional picture of me as I walk in my graduation exercises in 2015, where I had the honor of receiving my master's degree.

This pose reminds me of Errol Flynn, who lived many, many years ago. I resemble him with the mustache (and a couple shades darker).